The Tudors make me tic

Oliver Waite

BookLeaf Publishing

Presentation by *BookLeaf Publishing*

Web: www.bookleafpub.com

E-mail: info@bookleafpub.com

First edition 2021

PREFACE

I write on multiple platforms under the name The Tudors Make Me Tic. I use poetry and blogging as way of expressing myself, including my thoughts and feelings when I am unable to verbally find the words.

Poetry has seen me though some very dark times in life and I have found some comfort in this. Writing poems helps me understand the feelings better and enabled me to safely share those feelings with others.

You can find other blogs and poems across all social media platforms and on YouTube under the handle @TheTudorsMakeMeTic.

I hope you enjoy the journey with me whilst reading these poems. If you have any questions then feel free to message me on social media.

Thanks again,

Oliver

The tudors make me tic

The tudors make me tic.
And you and me click
We fit like gloves
For we are in love

Freedom

You're my freedom
But others don't see it that way
You're my freedom
But others think of you as a restriction.

You're my freedom
But others only see what I now can't do
You're my freedom
But others don't see the benefits.

You're my freedom:
less cuts and bruises.
You're my freedom:
less falls.

You're my freedom:
I can leave my flat.
You're my freedom:
less broken bones.

You're my freedom
But others see you as a negative
You're my freedom
But others think you have destroyed my life.

You're my freedom
But for others you're an embarrassment
You're my freedom
But others want you gone, openly tell me so.

You're my freedom:
less head injuries.
You're my freedom:
less pain and danger.

You're my freedom
My reason for less exhaustion.
You're my freedom
My reason I don't get stuck in public and have to crawl.

Yes, I can't hike up a mountain,
But without you I'd be stuck indoors.
I know you're not restricting me.
Without you, I’m restricted so much more.

And no, I've not given in!
I've done the opposite
by accepting
you're my freedom.

It's not my fault the world isn't designed for you.
That ramps and lifts might not be there.
That dropped kerbs are often blocked.

That places are often too narrow.

You're still my freedom.
The world just hasn't caught up yet.
You're my freedom.
You're my wheelchair.

Cats eyes

Snoring
Dad is breathing through a tube and mask
How strange
I really should ask

But instead
I'll sit on his head
Because I need my food
And it's gone 8 o'clock

He rises
At last!
I'll just sit by the bowl
So he doesn't forget

My cats eyes can see
That my bowl is still empty
Dad is sorting his meds,
I wait.

Now I've eaten
There's a whole day ahead
But really
I'm going back to bed

Where was this rule that I must be like you?

He, she, it.
You couldn't decide.
So I was all three
Or none at all

Tranny came next.
You insisted I was one,
You told me a tranny was a freak,
Just like me you said.

You whispered as I walked past
"What is it? A girl, no way it's a boy"
Except you never decided on boy or girl,
Freak and weirdo were what you deemed me.

Even those I called friend had a name for me
Goy
This weird combination of a boy and a girl
That's what they told me

Then peodphile,
Rapist,
Pervert
Were added to your collection

Every day for years and years,
So I started to believe the words,
Am I really that evil,
Will I turn out to be those things I asked myself daily

Freak and weirdo,
That's what I was to you,
Everyday you shouted all these words at me,
In fact every minute of everyday

Why so weird I would think to myself,
You laughed at my love for classical music
Called me freak for not having heard of your favourite pop artist
I never laughed when you hadn't heard of classical composers

Everything about me was wrong to you
It wasn't how I was supposed to be.
But how was I supposed to be I would think to myself,
Where was this rule that I must be like you?

Twice you tried to kill me,
I'm not even joking.
Cold blade of a saw against my neck.
A firework and lighter in my face "we'll blow you up" you yelled

You spat at me,
Punched me,
Tripped me
And kicked me

You stole my belongings
And laughed so hard when I got upset.
Then called me names,
When I wouldn't dare let you borrow my things.

You told me I should die
That everyone would be better with me dead.
I started to believe you,
Then I believed you so much I had to take action

I stole a few pills at a time
Collected them up
Then one night I took them all, wanting to die
I was 17.

When I woke up the next morning,
I was angry as hell
Because I couldn't deal with facing you

I couldn't do it anymore

There was one way I had managed to survive so far,
My skin flowed with red ink
A knife was my pen
Cutting myself open was the only way to survive.

At 18 I physically left you behind
Yet mentally you're always with me.
Belittering me all the time
I wonder if you even remember me?

My scarred mind and body certainly remember you all
You told me I should be dead so many times
And tried to kill me twice,
I've tried to kill me so many times more.

I'm still convinced I'll be evil
That evil person you said I was
I'm reminded of it all the time
Your words are in my mind everyday and I wonder

Will I ever be free?

Henry

Ah Henry
What can I say?
For you I love to play

From Mozart to Strauss
Beethoven, Poulenc and even Gliere
Or The dream of the rhinoceros.

French horn,
Loved since I was born
Oh Henry you are my forte.

Drawing

Drawing

Drawing lines

Lines of red

Like an artist

But my paper

Is my own skin

And my pen

My own knife

Six

The musical is Six
Oh where can I get my fix

Tudor queens
Wives of a certain king

Pop princesses
In fabulous dresses

Singing in rhymes
About their so called crimes

It's their story to tell
About how they fell

Rewriting history
Or is it really her-story

In another world

Hearing voices, hallucinations.
Being tracked by the government.
Seeing death, and a circus.
I can smell the dentist.
In another world.
Being poisoned.
I am watched.
Malcolm.
Scared.

Through a mesh above the window sill

The only fresh air I feel,
Is through a mesh above the window sill.
I hear the bird song and the breeze.
Even felt the sun on my back with ease.

But I'm so far away from it all.
Locked in here waiting to fall.
And it is getting harder everyday.
To find a way through or another way.

You see, I have plans of a kind.
The type others don't like to find.
So I am sectioned here.
Not able to leave, to go anywhere.

My mind is as noisy as fuck.
The complete opposite to a rubber duck.
Voices I hear, and clowns I see.
Even the television talks to me.

Visiting the circus has not been fun.
I have even heard the sound of guns.
Trapped in here I can't get away.
And it only gets harder everyday.

Thirty minutes outside a day.
That's all I am allowed by the way.
Staff watch me everywhere.
An escape is no where.

For I am locked in here, against my will.
You must understand the struggle is real.
The only fresh air I feel,
Is through a mesh above the window sill.

Seymour and Aragon

Seymour and Aragon
What can I say.
Two cats I have
Who are here to stay.

Named after queens
You are royalty to me.
Mr moo and little one
The nicknames of fun.

For you really are weird.
Crazy as can be.
But therefore
You really do fit in with me.

Seymour licks sellotape
And Aragon skin.
Both love a straw
But not from the bin.

But what do you love most of all
For it must be sleep as that's all you do.

Except at 3am
when the zoomies take hold.

You are scamps, cheeky
silly and cute.
But ultimately loved
You life saving pets.

Tap. Tap. Tap.

Tap. Tap. Tap.

Tap. Tap. Tap.

Tap. Tap. Tap.

Done correctly? I silently ask my brain
A response screams no
Not a voice
But the thoughts remain
So of course I didn't do it correctly
I never do.

Tap. Tap. Tap.

Tap. Tap. Tap.

Tap. Tap. Tap.

Correct now?
The same response,
Of course, why would I have done it correctly.

But my head is louder
Now I can see what will happen if I don't do it correctly
Desperate I go again.

Tap. Tap. Tap.

Tap. Tap. Tap.

Tap. Tap. Tap.

Three sets of three done three times,
Surely that gives me a little time.
It does, but for how long I think.
Thoughts of causing a train crash may have reduced,
But I am a ticking bomb
Waiting for the next obsession.

There it is.
A switch turned on with no plug in its socket.
Immediately I go to turn it off
But I wonder will switching it off be enough
Words 'fire' 'your fault' circle my brain
Rushing to the switch to get them gone.

Click.

It makes that perfect sound,
As if resetting my brain for a few moments again.
Giving myself a moment to think,
As I know I won't get long.
It never is long at all.
A few minutes if I am lucky.

Another switch turned on,
This time my brain is louder.
I don't want people to die
I rush to the switch
Hoping it is a one switch job.
I fear it isn't as i begin to see flames.

Click.

It wasn't right,
I know straight away
Can't tell you how or why.
I just know.
Now my head is full of flames
I am scared.

Click. Click. Click.

Click. Click. Click.

Click. Click. Click.

Three sets of three don't work
The switch is back to on.
I sit,
looking at the switch
To an onlooker just staring at it
As if pointlessly

One. Two. Three.

One. Two. Three.

One. Two. Three.

One. Two. Three.

One. Two. Three.

One. Two. Three.

One. Two. Three.

One. Two. Three.

One. Two. Three.

Click.

It works.
The flames retreat.
I breathe for a moment.
Trying to let my heart settle down.
And my palms dry.
All the while knowing it will start again in a moment.

Constantly I am
Checking
Counting
Tapping
Turning off
Turning on
Lining up
Moving.

Constantly, constantly.

You won't know this,
But today I have been

A murderer,

A rapist,
A peodphile,
An arsonist,
A terroist,
Infectious
Diseased
A liar

And tomorrow I'll be the same.
The next week,
Fortnight,
Month,
Year.
I'll be the same.

So I will always be

Checking
Counting
Tapping

Turning off
Turning on
Clicking

Moving
Lining up
Rearranging

Always
Because if I don't
Those moments of quiet I get
I'll never, ever get.
So I will tap, check, count
As much as I need.
Because I am desperate for the moments of quiet.
Desperate for my brain to stop telling myself I'm a monster.
Really fucking desperate.

Tap. Tap. Tap.

Tap. Tap. Tap.

Tap. Tap. Tap.

Tap. Tap. Tap.

Tap. Tap. Tap.

Tap. Tap. Tap.

Tap. Tap. Tap.

Tap. Tap. Tap.

Tap. Tap. Tap.

World mental health day

It's world mental health day
So what can I say.
It's a day to declare
That everyone does care.

Except is that really the truth
Or are they really just Ruth-less
Because you see
On this day to just be

When I reach out
All they say is 'don't shout'
We have no beds,
Nothing for your head.

For I am mentally ill
To the public though not civil.
Schizophrenic you see
And complex PTSD.

Reach out they say
Except there is no way

Non speaking I am
phones is the only way they can

In a world that should be accessible
Is this acceptable?

Not your joke

My neck snaps back,
Sudden.
Quick.

Simultaneously: my left calf tenses.
My eyes blink.
My eyebrows raise.

My shoulder raises.
Fingers jumping about.
My neck suddenly flicks to the side and I feel a click and pain.

My jaw clenches.
Now my neck is constantly nodding.
Stomach clenches, pain shoots through my body.

Legs kick out.
Feet,
And toes start to jump about.

Now my right arm won't stay still.
Oh shit, I punched my head! Thrice!
My finger flips up at an unaware passerby.

The sniffing won't stop.
I've not got a cold.
And, no blowing my nose doesn't help!

Random words come out.
Some end up forming sentences.
I say the strangest of things.

'You've got a chicken on your head'
'Fuck off'
'I love boomerangs'

The time all this happens in?
I'd say 5-10 seconds.
On repeat constantly 24/7, only the content changes.

I'm exhausted.
My muscles ache.
And I'm in pain.

Tourette's
My reality

Not your joke.

To you it's nothing

To you it's nothing
You say ok, don't worry
To you it's nothing
You can easily adapt

To you it's nothing
Hardly a change at all
To me it's everything
I have to readjust and re-plan

To you it's nothing
To me it's anxiety
To me it's anger
To me it's fear

To you it's nothing
You say 'stuff changes all the time get used to it'
But my life is based on routines and plans,
To try and navigate an inaccessible world

To you it's nothing
To you my anxiety is over the top
To you my anger is misdirected
To you my shutdown is wrong

To you it's nothing
I want you to know I'm not angry at you
I want you to know my anxiety isn't voluntary
I want you to know I wish it could be nothing to me too

Big
Small
Rare
Everyday
Random
One aspect
All aspects
Sudden
Planned

There is no difference to me
They are all change
All change that reduces me to an anxious wreck
All change that fuels me with anger and cause me to meltdown

To you it's nothing
To me it can wreck a day, week or month
To you it's nothing
To me it's uncontrollable fear

I'm not ignorant to know nothing changes
New five pound notes I've not touched yet

Phone updates that cause meltdowns
Shops rearranging that can leave me non-verbal for weeks

I know people get ill, emergencies happen, work shifts change.
So I'm never angry at you.
I'm angry at change.
Please believe me I know they are separate.

If I change plans myself
Know I've not done so lightly
The same feelings haunt me inside
As when others change plans.

To you it's nothing
To me it's so much more.
Trying to process the new information and work out what to do.
This isn't a quick process at all.

My ability to cope with change
Will not change
But I really do wish a change of plan or a new five pound note,
Could be manageable.

So when to you it's nothing
Or hardly anything at all

Remember for me,
Everything is falling apart and I'm doing my best.

Ate away my sanity

Stigmas
Stereotypes
Consequences
Do I say?
Do I tell?

Do I mention the things that cannot be seen.
Do I speak the things they do not know.
My mind debates, it talks, and squirms.

I want to break down barriers
Not be held back by stigmas
But my mind is an ever lasting shriek
Scared like hell of the consequences.

You see the thing is I am:
Mad
Crazy
Bonkers
Batshit
Insane
Nutty
Mental

You see that's the thing do I say or not.

For years it was a secret,
No one knew.
I allowed my mind to eat itself alive.
I devoured my own brain.
Ate away my sanity.

You see I am mentally ill
I will say it now, but the damage of secrets is
done.
Folk think I am so incredibly open,
Yet 89% of my mind is closed off to the public.
It stays under wraps,
Maybe one item goes on display
Yet really I am a secret waiting to explode.
Waiting for that whistleblower moment.
Yet I do not think it will come.

You see the stigma is so strong.
The consequences are so scary.
So I will take my whole truth to the grave.
Where the silence will devour it forever.

Sections

Locked away
Days,
Weeks,
Months go by and never allowed outside.

Rights taken off you.
Medication forced upon you.
Clothes stripped off you.
Possessions hidden away from you.

Yelled at,
Abused,
Bullied,
Threatened.

Constantly watched,
Lights always on.
Never can sleep,
Nothing to eat.

Forced to talk,
Even though the words fail.
Called names.
Jokes made at your expense.

Nothing to do,
Except stare at walls.
Plotting your escape
Is all you live for.

Alarms pulled
Restrained.
With joints twisted up behind your back.
Then suddenly head against the cold floor.
Held down by 4 men, and medication injected.

Made to go to meetings.
You're discussed, but your voice is not important.
They talk numbers and debate what to do with you,
As you sit there rocking.

You're a list of diagnosis.
They tut as they hear BPD.
And then they question if you are faking for attention.
You scream 'no', yet all that does is cause an alarm to ring and pound your ears.

You need to go outside.
But until you're deemed 'good enough'
No chance!

Trapped inside as the days and nights become one.

Drugged up
Like a zombie
You shuffle around,
As do the other patients.

You are expected to survive this.
You are expected to not want to run away.
You are expected to remain calm.
'How can I?' I think.
For I am in living hell and I can't cope.

Sectioned.
That's what it's really like, a living hell.

Dear William

Some will laugh
Call me names
Tell me I am silly
To have a teddy bear

But you are so dear to me
My safety and my sanity
Cuddle you every night
And tell you how hard I fight

You have been with me through everything
Every battle that I've faced
The good times and the bad.
You never make me sad

You've seen my most fragile moments
As I've held you when I tried to die
And I've hugged you as I've wept with joy
You've helped through the sections 2 and 3

You helped to protect the girl I was
And you've helped to shape the man I am
For dear William
You are truly a star

Malcolm

You are a silent whisper
A silent scream
The man who haunts me
The man who tells me to die.

You are vicious
A nasty voice
The man I cannot escape
The man who is with me everywhere.

You are clever
A manipulative voice
The man who makes me cut open my arm
The man who makes me tie the noose.

You are Malcolm
A voice so loud, a man so visible
Yet only to me
For no one else has ever seen or heard you.

My own constant hell

Eyes squeezed tight shut.
Hands clamped over my ears.
Hiding in a corner far from them all.
Taking short, shallow breaths.
I rock and rock but it does not help.
Where am I, you ask.
'Sensory hell' I reply.

Curtains shut.
Lights off.
Sunglasses on.
Eyes clenched shut.
Yet still too bright.
A searing pain through my head.
Eyes burning like volcanic lava.

'I can't eat that,' I tell you.
'Why on earth not?'
I debate in my head to tell the truth or lie.
I am brave.
'The texture makes my heart pound
my mouth burn

and I want to scratch my tongue out'
'Don't be ridiculous, it is soft.'
I put it in my mouth and immediately
it's sensory hell.

My ears are pounding.
I want to scratch them off.
I am being beaten repeatedly on my ear drum.
Yet you don't see that.
I yelp and cover my ears.
Ears which already have ear plugs in.
Yet the beating continues, I'll never be free.

Smoke
A bath bomb
Aftershave
Cleaning products.
I smelt one.
I smelt them all at once,
and now my head pounds and nausea rises
within.

You reject that this sensory hell exists.
Yet question why I'm unwell.
You question my sunglasses indoors,
my noise cancelling ear plugs,
my need for breaks.
Yet never stop to think that I'm in bloody agony
constantly

from the world.
Welcome to my sensory hell.

So are you really my ally?

Do not call Trump a crazy psycho,
And then come to me as my ally.
Citing famous words of
'I am here for you'
Because could you bare my crazy psycho reality.

Do not cheer on May and her Tories,
And then come to me as an ally.
Quoting famous words of
'Reach out, tell your GP'
Because there are services being slashed left right and centre
Money being stripped away.

So who exactly do I reach out to?
Because it's not you
And it's not the services no more
So tell me please.
Are you really there for my crazy, mad, psycho reality

Or are you just quoting the same old thing
because it's easy to say
'I am here if you need me'

So are you really my ally?

I know

You told me to
wear make up
like popular music
wear dresses and skirts
drink alcohol
not talk about history
keep still
keep quiet
talk less
talk more
make eye contact
not meltdown
not tic
smile more
be happy
not be anxious
be sociable
not stim
not talk about classical music
act neurotypical

So I tried it all
I tried so damn hard
You see I didn't want to be the one who was
tormented and alone

so I tried it all to fit in how you wanted me to.

I wanted to be liked
I wanted a few friends
But the friends I made were fake as they knew a fake me.
They also didn't care.

I know I'm different and that's ok
I know I'm liked as me.
The friendships I have now are genuine
as I'm no longer faking who I am.

I know I'm different and that's ok
I'm a non-binary trans man and that's ok

I'm asexual and gay and that's ok

I'm mentally ill and that's ok

I have Tourette's and that's ok

I'm autistic and that's ok

I'm a wheelchair user and that's ok

I'm an AAC user and that's ok

I'm disabled and that's ok

I know my special interest is the Tudor period
and that's ok

I love classical music and that's ok

I stim and that's ok

I have sensory overloads and that's ok

I have meltdowns and that's ok

I know I love history and that's ok

I don't want to drink alcohol and that's ok

I love my beard and that's ok

I know my limits and that's ok

I know I can't cope with many things
and that's ok.

Every time you told me to fit in
to avoid being the bullied, abused person with
no friends
I believed you
but any friends I had weren't true friends who
cared.

I know now that I can be myself
completely myself
and people like me.
I know that adults lie to young people who aren't
'the norm'
Because you all lied to me.

I know I'm different

and that's ok
I now know
I don't need to fit in to have friends
I also know I'm not less
just because I'm different.

www.ingramcontent.com/pod-product-compliance
Lightning Source LLC
Chambersburg PA
CBHW051738130826
49812CB00033B/918
9789357448079